DIY Crafts

*10 Sophisticated DIY
Craft Ideas
to Make and Sell
or Give to Friends*

by Bonnie Stevens

Table of Contents

Introduction 1

Chapter 1: Photo Transfers and Polaroid Transfers. 11

Chapter 2: Chalkboard Frames 17

Chapter 3: Candy Necklaces and Bracelets 19

Chapter 4: Teacup Candles 23

Chapter 5: Choker Necklaces 27

Chapter 6: Beadie Babies 31

Chapter 7: Tie Dye Clothing 35

Chapter 8: Dried Flower Sachets and Charms 41

Conclusion 47

Introduction

Do you have a little extra time on your hands, enjoy arts and crafts, and want to impress your friends and/or make a bit of extra money? If you've always dreamed of selling goods or crafts online or at your local market or fair, this book is for you. The same goes if you're sick of what stores have to offer and want to learn how to make your own unique gifts or trinkets to give out as gifts or party favors.

There are a myriad of different project ideas you could come up with depending on where your interests may lie, as well as those of your friends and your current market. This book is a collection of a wide spectrum of craft ideas that will result in quality products that are nice enough to give away as gifts, or even sell.

You can either follow the directions provided, or you can use this information as "inspiration" and think outside the box even further without limiting yourself to how you go about executing the projects. It's my suggestion that you first try it as explained, and then brainstorm about how you might like to do it differently next time. I believe it's always good to give yourself the freedom to experiment, and think about your own creative variations so as to contribute to the 'uniqueness' of the things you produce. The more you experiment, the more your crafts will stand out, and that's an important feature if you plan on selling. In this book, I have tried my best to be as explicit as possible in describing my ways of doing things. I have also tried to include activities for every skill level, taste and budget.

Before we get to the items you'll be learning to make, I have one more piece of advice: As you move your items into the marketplace, try and find your niche, or the area that you feel you could be the most talented or specialized in. Even if this is really only a hobby or a way to make some extra pocket money on the side for you, the more specialized you become, the more recognizable and consistent you will be within your marketplace.

If you do decide to make more than one type of item, be sure that the style is at least somewhat consistent so that customers will recognize your work over and over again. This way, you stand a chance at making more money. Furthermore, if you ever decide that the crafts you're making are more than a hobby to you and you would like them to blossom into a part time or full time business, you won't have to work very hard to successfully give yourself a cohesive brand.

Now with all that said, let's get started! Here's a brief overview of the products you'll be learning to make:

- **Photo transfer onto wood.** These are great, especially if you are a professional artist and you want to branch out a bit. "Reusing" and "Upcycling" are becoming incredibly popular right now, and for good reason. Plus, wood, especially if it's beat up or textured, gives so much more character to photos. Just make sure that as you select or shoot photos to transfer onto wood, you pick ones that will look great on that texture. This may require some experimentation and trial and error on your part before you get it right.

- **Polaroid lifts/transfers.** This project is along the same vein as the one above, except that it's even more "professional" looking, although it is also slightly more difficult. The result can be stunning, and since Polaroid cameras are becoming all the rage again, why not make the most of them? If you've never used a Polaroid camera before, now would be the time. You can easily find them (inexpensively) online or at trendy stores like Urban Outfitters. And the film, in Fujifilm form, is also available online via photo stores, in Urban Outfitters, or at The Impossible

Project. Another fun, variant idea is just to take Polaroid photos of your customers at craft markets, with their permission, of course. A Polaroid is a fun souvenir for any customer and their friends and family, as well as a quick way to make an easy buck.

- **Chalkboard frames**. If you love, love, love, ornate or quirky antique frames as much as I do, then this project will tickle your fancy. And when you sell it, of course, you should throw in some chalk for your customers as a part of the package deal.

- **Homemade candy jewelry.** These are sure to be a crowd favorite among customers and friends who have small children, and you can make them *so* much more attractive, unique, and interesting than those chalky sweet tart necklaces found at the grocery store. Another variation is the colorful, fun, chunky, and surprisingly wearable jellybean bracelet.

- **Teacup candles.** Now granted, you could make candles in any container that you like, but my personal favorite is the teacup because it's so delicate and unique, and I think it's so much fun to look for cute matched or mismatched teacup sets at thrift stores and flea markets. If you can, I would even suggest trying to find teacups that still have saucers, just to complete the look. An alternative to this (and it's really all based on preference of the look you like) would be Mason jars. These are also fun, easy to find cheaply, and in abundance.

- **Beadie Babies.** You can bring back the 90s with these popular beaded creatures — the other 90s favorite and alternative to Beanie Babies. If you grew up in the 80s or 90s, I'm sure the skill will come back to you quickly, and the product will appeal to you, your nostalgic peers, and their children, who have likely never seen one before.

- **Choker necklaces**. Let's face it. Chokers are back in a big way and they can really be made however you want. I'm going to show you how to make my favorite version using lace.

- **Lavender sachets.** These are so easy to make, and so soothing; you could sell these on their own, or include them as bonuses with larger purchases as a small "thanks for shopping" gift.

- **Dried flower and herb charms.** In looks, these remind me a lot of the sachets, except you can't smell them. Dried flowers and herbs look lovely as charms; dried and put into little corked bottles or in a glass or resin pendant, which you can purchase premade or make yourself using molds. And if you aren't into the whole necklace and/or jewelry-making thing, I have found that people will pay for the bottles of dried flowers themselves.

- **Tie dye clothing.** Especially if you're planning on selling at markets, these can be cool to make on the spot. Everyone loves them, from small children to adults, and you can even make it an interactive activity, having your customers and/or friends help you make them.

With these ideas in mind, let's get started! A quick note: You'll notice the order the crafts are chronicled in the book thematically, rather than in the same order as listed above. Not to worry though, they're all here!

© Copyright 2015 by Miafn LLC - All rights reserved.

This document is geared towards providing reliable information in regards to the topic and issue covered. The publication is sold with the idea that the publisher is not required to render accounting, officially permitted, or otherwise, qualified services. If advice is necessary, legal or professional, a practiced individual in the profession should be ordered.

- From a Declaration of Principles which was accepted and approved equally by a Committee of the American Bar Association and a Committee of Publishers and Associations.

In no way is it legal to reproduce, duplicate, or transmit any part of this document in either electronic means or in printed format. Recording of this publication is strictly prohibited and any storage of this document is not allowed unless with written permission from the publisher. All rights reserved.

The information provided herein is stated to be truthful and consistent, in that any liability, in terms of inattention or otherwise, by any usage or abuse of any policies, processes, or directions contained within is solely and completely the responsibility of the recipient reader. Under no circumstances will any legal responsibility or blame be held against the publisher for any reparation, damages, or monetary loss due to the information herein, either directly or indirectly.

Respective authors own all copyrights not held by the publisher.

The information herein is offered for informational purposes solely, and is universal as so. The presentation of the information is without contract or any type of guarantee assurance.

The trademarks that are used are without any consent, and the publication of the trademark is without permission or backing by the trademark owner. All trademarks and brands within this book are for clarifying purposes only and are the owned by the owners themselves, not affiliated with this document.

Chapter 1: Photo Transfers and Polaroid Transfers

This is one of my favorite projects, if not my favorite, aside from the sachets and flower charms we're going to talk about later on. I'm a photographer, and as such, I know that there are a lot of photographs for sale at craft fairs. Some of them are great, some excellent, some not so much; but often shoppers can get a bit lost among the sea of choices and give up. One of the ways to make your photos stand out is to transfer them. Now, transfers can be done onto a lot of surfaces, but I prefer wood for the feel of its natural grain, and that's what we're going to talk about here.

You will need:

- Photos

- A piece of wood (lighter is great to start with, and I prefer found wood, which will require a little more effort to sand down but looks cooler. It's really up to you.)

- Photoshop or other image editing software programs

- Access to a laser printer (inkjet would work, but the image might run a bit when it's wet). You can always visit a printing center such as Kinkos, Staples, or Office Depot and use the laser printers there for mere pennies.

- Scissors and a bone folder

- Matte gel medium

- Mod Podge

- Two brushes

- A rag

- Paper towels or an old towel you don't mind ruining.

Print out your photo of choice. Check that the resolution of your image is 300 dpi so it won't look all grainy when printed. Also, fit the photo to the approximate dimensions of the wood. If you have a funky shaped piece and need to trim some off, that's okay. It just adds to the uniqueness and as you'll learn to get better at judging odd-shaped pieces. Print your image on a fairly thin type of paper, such as 24 lb.

Cut out your printed photo and thinly coat it with a layer of matte gel medium. A thin coat is ideal because you don't want it to glob up or make your photo run.

Put the gelled photo face down onto the wood. Remember, you aren't gluing the photo to the surface; you're transferring it, that's why it needs to be face down. Use the bone folder to make sure it's all flat, no bubbles, and nothing gets wonky. Then let dry before continuing to the next step. It's going to take at least eight hours.

Once it's dry, take a damp towel and soak your wood. Remember to wring it out. It shouldn't be soaking-wet. Let it sit for a while, and start rubbing until all the excess paper fibers come off. You can also use your fingers; it just depends on the look you want to achieve. Now you're going to let it dry again. If you notice it's still a little fuzzy, you can always rewet it.

Finally, it's time for Mod Podge, which acts like a sealant or finish. And you're done.

Quick tip: The only difference between using an inkjet or a laser printer for this project is that clear film may work best as transfer paper for inkjet. You can find this at any photo store. Just experiment and see what works best for you.

Now let's talk about Polaroid Transfers. This project has essentially the same end goal, but it's a little different because you're using Polaroid as your transfer material as opposed to a printed out photo. I think this makes it that much more awesome because each one will be unique. So get to snapping some Polaroids, and let's get started.

Aside from your film, you need:

- One medium bowl of cold AND hot water
- Watercolor paper
- Scissors
- A small knife
- Small paintbrushes
- Tweezers

Cut off the border of your image, you will see that you can pull the actual image away from its backing. Peel until you're left with just your image. Trim the edges down.

Soak your film in hot water. I mean boiling-hot water. As the photo wrinkles, it means you're almost good to go. Just watch the image. It should take around five to ten minutes. Keeping the photo submerged, use your hand and the knife to carefully peel back the top layer. This part takes much time and patience. Clean the thin part of your image that is left over carefully. You may see some residue come off. Then, move the image to the cold water. Float your watercolor paper beneath the image in the cold water, and as you flatten the image, press it against the paper. Don't worry if it isn't completely flat. Part of the beauty of Polaroid transfers are the wrinkles and shapes they make. If you really like this look, you can even use your fingers to push the polaroids into abstract shapes.

Lift the paper out, and you're finished. Now it just needs to dry for a day. And like the laser or inkjet images, these can be transferred onto any surface you like; it just takes some practice.

Chapter 2: Chalkboard Frames

This is one of the simplest projects in the book.

You will need:

- Frames. You'll find the most interesting ones at flea markets and antique shops.

- Paint that works for the material that the frame is made of.

- Chalkboard paint. This is going to turn the glass surface of the frame into a chalkboard. You can find this at any arts and crafts store, or order it online.

Paint the frames as you see fit, with any design or other embellishments, of course you will need glue for that.

Paint the glass with chalkboard paint. I would suggest doing these two steps separately, and allowing them to dry in between. Sell or gift your new chalkboard frames with pieces of colorful chalk.

Chapter 3: Candy Necklaces and Bracelets

You know the candy necklaces you see in grocery stores? Did you know that you can make even cooler ones at home? Not only are these great for small children and as inexpensive birthday party favors, but also I think they'd be a hit at your local market. Depending on how advanced you want to get with it, they can actually be pretty chic, especially if you make a cuff out of jellybeans.

One of the easiest ways to make candy jewelry is to select candy that already have holes in it, like Twizzlers, peach rings, Sour Punch Straws, etc. Just string them together and you're done. If you're looking for something a bit more refined, try jellybeans and sweet tarts. All you need is a very small needle, which you will use to pierce the candy with. It may take some practice, and you might have quite a few break on you. For either choice of candy, you'll want to use a very thin stretch cord. Nothing too thick or the hole made by the needle will not be big enough. As you go, make sure you wipe off your needle, or else it will get too sticky to work with. The same thing is true for the sweet tarts. Make sure you leave a bit of cord at the end to knot up so it won't fall off.

And that's it! Now anyone, children or adults, can have edible, wearable, sugary jewelry.

Chapter 4: Teacup Candles

This craft is so much fun to me, and I actually own quite a few myself. I love, love, love teacups, and this project is definitely much more fun if you find some cool or sweet vintage patterns. Don't go to Ikea; check out your local flea market or antique store first. It's usually cheaper that way too.

You will need:

- Teacups of your choice
- Wax (flakes work best)
- Wooden skewers
- Tape
- Scissors
- Stove
- Double boiler
- Bowl
- Oven mitts
- Hot plate
- Wicks

- Color dye

- Scent of your choice

First you need a wick support, which you can make by taping two skewers together parallel to one another with the wick in the middle. The wooden sticks will balance across the top of the cup so that the wick will stand up in the cup. You can use a string dipped in wax as a wick.

Fill up your boiler and put it on the stove to heat. Place your bowl in the boiler (it should be heat safe, most likely glass) into the water. Add your wax and it will begin to melt.

As the wax flakes melt, you can add in whatever color and/or scent you like. Lift your melted wax from the water and wipe the bottom of the bowl dry. You can now pour it into your teacups; be careful to not spill any wax onto your wooden skewers. Leave about a quarter inch of cup space showing at the top. You may also have to hold onto the skewers to keep them in place.

Let your wax dry. I would suggest checking back every few hours. Finally, you'll need to trim your wick down to where it is held in place by the skewers. And now you can use, sell, or gift your fab candles.

Chapter 5: Choker Necklaces

Choker necklaces are back in style, from the tattoo choker to the simple lace choker. If you really like making jewelry or necklaces, I would suggest exploring all of these options, but in this book, I'm just going to teach you how to make a simple lace or metal choker.

Lace chokers are a lovely interactive product you can make in front of your customers. Actually, I believe making them in front of customers makes the process simpler because you can make sure that the necklace is the correct length for their neck. Not only that, they can also pick the kind of lace they prefer.

All you need is:

- Lace of your choice

- Clasp of your choice (you can find little flat ones that are perfect for clamping onto the ends of lace)

- Basic jewelry making tools, such as scissors and a clamp to secure the clasp onto the lace.

I find that broad, flat lace works best, especially at the clasp end, but lace that looks like a daisy chain is also very popular. Measure your lace against the client's neck (or use your own for reference, leaving a little extra, because it's easier to trim some off and put the clasp back on than to make a new one if it's too short). Then put your clasp on, leaving some extra on the chain so your customers or friends can hook it longer if they like.

The second kind of choker involves a premade wire base. On this wire base, you can build it up with decoupage or just add on your favorite charms or beads. Again, these are easy to make in front of your client.

If you have more experience in jewelry-making, then you could also consider adding a jump ring and a crystal or charm of your choice, which is extremely popular now.

Chapter 6: Beadie Babies

Beadie babies are a 90s classic that I totally support bringing back. They're incredibly simple to make. All you need is:

- String—a thicker cotton string works best

- Pony beads in different sizes and colors depending on your preference and the pattern you're using

- A pattern—one Internet search is all you need to find thousands of patterns, ranging from beginner to advanced. (Just as with learning any new craft, I would suggest starting off with more simple designs.)

- A key ring, since they make great key rings.

I have provided you with some sites for patterns below, which will provide you with the exact number and color of pony beads as well as the appropriate amount of string. They also provide special instructions, such as when a Beadie Baby needs whiskers or feelers, etc.

Some sites for Beadie Baby patterns are:

- Beadiecritters.com

- http://www.dltk-kids.com/pokemon/pokemon_beadie_critters.htm

- http://www.beadedflowers.info/about/about_bead_buddies.php

Chapter 7: Tie Dye Clothing

Tie-dye is so simple and awesome that anyone can figure it out. All you need is clothing dye that is suitable for washing, some t-shirts, and rubber bands. Now, some dyes are made for natural materials while others are made for manmade materials; and unless you are very experienced in the art of tie dying, I would suggest sticking to the natural ones. These include cotton or linen, which is made from cotton. While you can tie-dye anything, if you're looking for something simple to start with, I would suggest getting a pack of shirts from Wal-Mart or Target. If you want to step up your game later on, you can always get some higher quality shirts, such as those made by American Apparel. While they do include some polyester in some of their shirts, keep in mind that as long as it's fifty percent or under, you should be okay with natural dye.

Lots of companies specialize in dyes, such as Tulip, Rit, or Dharma. All of these companies offer premixed dye kits, all you only need to add is cold water. The same goes for dye packets. If you do decide to mix your own dye, make sure you get all the necessary ingredients to mix it properly. These ingredients and other items include:

- Dye
- Rubber bands and gloves
- Squeeze bottles for dye
- Urea
- Soda ash
- Rubber bands
- Anything to keep your workspace clean and tidy, such as rags, paper towels, or a drop cloth.

First you will soak the shirt in warm water and soda ash for about ten minutes, which performs what is called sizing on the garment. This is where you make sure the shirt is going to allow the dye to properly adhere, and this will also ensure it will not shrink and change the design afterwards.

Next, you'll wring your shirt out to ensure all the excess moisture is expelled. I grasp the shirt then twist it down and around a dowel rod to achieve that perfect swirled shape we all love. However, you can always just skip straight to the rubber-banding phase if you like. With practice, you'll be able to see what patterns you can achieve, and if you're too impatient to experiment, you could also look online and see what other techniques and patterns you may find.

After the shirt has been banded, it's time to add the dye. When mixing dyes, make sure you follow the instructions and add any necessary ingredients, such as water or urea, as instructed. Decide where you want the dye to go on the shirt. For best results, plan it out, that way you don't get any icky brownish-looking spots in the middle. With red, yellow, and blue, you can create any color you want with careful planning.

Now, this is the part that we never knew about as kids. For best results, you should put your banded shirt in a plastic bag (or somehow seal it and cover it with plastic) and let it sit for at least eight hours, up to thirty six hours. I guess it just depends on your patience and the result you want to get. Don't really leave it longer than thirty six hours though, or it may begin to look a bit funky.

When you remove it from the bag, wear rubber gloves and rinse the shirt out under running water. Lukewarm is fine, as usual.

Hang your shirt up to dry, and you're done.

Once your shirt is dry you can also choose to cut off the sleeves, shred the back, add lace, safety pins, or beads to the shreds, anything you can think of. Or, if you like it better as is, just leave it as is.

Chapter 8: Dried Flower Sachets and Charms

Of all the items here, I think that this is the simplest, but also my favorite. As I've mentioned in the previous chapter on transfers, people love the idea of using natural things and recycling their arts and crafts. Flower sachets and charms do both of these things. I also think that this is a good craft for people who already enjoy gardening and have gardens. If you've never considered selling your herbs and flowers before, this is a cool way to start. Now, if you don't have your own garden, I would definitely suggest starting one before trying to make and sell these two particular crafts. I say that because if you were to try and make them with store bought herbs and flowers, it would quickly become too expensive to be anything other than the occasional gift, and while that's okay, it's best not to limit yourself.

Now, assuming you do have a small garden, here's what you do:

For both the sachets and charms, you want to select flowers and herbs that are going to hold up well during the drying process. Keep in mind that this does not mean you can't use delicate flowers; it simply means that you may have to learn to be more patient than initially preferred or expected. Rather than the traditional method of flower-drying we all learned as kids (pressing flowers between the book pages), I have learned that there are two better methods to ensuring the plants still look beautiful at the end. And the best part is that with these methods, you aren't running the risk of your plants or flowers retaining too much moisture and turning brown.

The methods are:

- With a bunch of plants, wick off any extra moisture, and tie them together in a bunch by the stems. Find an area in your house that is warm and dry. I would suggest the kitchen or maybe even an attic if it doesn't get too hot. Find somewhere to hang them from. While you can build something especially for this purpose, I would recommend finding existing beams or hooks in your house to make less work for yourself. Hang the plants upside down to allow them to dry. If you've never done this before, keep in mind that different plants may have different drying rates. Also remember that you just want the plants to be dry, but not brittle, to the touch. So I'd say just check on them every half day or so. In my experience, with smaller plants such as rosemary and lavender, they dry quickly, within two days.

- The other method, if you're just drying enough plants for a bottle or a sachet or two, is to dry the plants in a shallow bowl or saucer out in the sun. Of course, depending on the season, this may take longer. I would also suggest bringing your sprigs in at night if there is a forecast for rain. If it's winter or you aren't currently getting much sun, you could try using plant lamps for this purpose, which also provide some heat.

The plants you're going to choose to dry are going to depend on their purpose. For the sachets, you want the focus to be on smell and the soothing, calming, or energizing properties of a plant. You could use pure lavender, or rose hips, maybe even marigold. Also consider including things like dried orange peel or cardamom pods. Change up your recipes according to the season or according to what you think a specific friend or customer might benefit from.

For the charms, the plants you choose will all be based on look and color scheme, because you are putting them into a clear bottle for the customer or a friend to wear. I have found that tiny wildflowers or lavender pair well with larger flowers such as pansies, roses or marigold. When drying for charms, try to think about how big your bottle or pendant base is, because that's really going to determine the size of the flower you can use. And remember that for larger flowers such as lilies or hibiscuses, you can always pull off one petal or even the stamen to use as opposed to using the entire flower.

Though you can buy premade sachets, charms, and bottles to put your dried plants in, I think it's much more fun and unique to make them yourself.

The sachets should be packaged in a material that is semi-transparent at the very least, so that you can still enjoy the look and feel of the contents inside. I would also suggest a breathable material, such as a light, loosely woven cotton linen or cotton muslin. I really hate the feel of artificial fabrics that store bought sachets often come in because they also don't breathe well, which is the whole purpose of a sachet. You should definitely get the scent as you are packaging them. They're perfect for putting in sock drawers or under pillows.

As for the charms, buy fresh corks for those, but see if you can find tiny vintage bottles to put the contents in. They'll come in all shapes, sizes and textures, and are a lot more fun to hunt for. EBay is good for things like this, but also check out your local thrift store for great finds. You just have to be dedicated in finding them, but to me that's half the fun.

Finally, when you sell these crafts, it might be a good idea to make both premade sachets and bottles for the market, but you could also give your customers the option of customizing their own. Just lay out your bottles for them to select from, and have a little tray for all the different kinds of flowers, herbs or spices you have for them to choose from. It will be fun for them to watch you make their custom piece.

Conclusion

Now you know how to make a variety of crafts, from teacup candles to a tie-dye t-shirts. However, don't stop here, continue to explore and see what you'd like to make. As you start out with these crafts, I recommend giving them as gifts to your friends, but as you get better, you can always consider taking them to your local crafts fair.

No matter what you do, try to make these products with the utmost quality and care. Just because they are easy to make doesn't mean that it doesn't take time and effort to make them well and beautifully. Take your time, but most of all; enjoy yourself.

Finally, I'd like to thank you for purchasing this book! If you enjoyed it or found it helpful, I'd greatly appreciate it if you'd take a moment to leave a review on Amazon. Thank you!

Printed in Great Britain
by Amazon